Baseball Stars

Virginia Buckman

HIGH
interest
books

Children's Press®
A Division of Scholastic Inc.
New York / Toronto / London / Auckland / Sydney
Mexico City / New Delhi / Hong Kong
Danbury, Connecticut

Book Design: Dean Galiano
Contributing Editor: Geeta Sobha

Photo Credits: Cover, p. 4 © Dilip Vishwanat/Getty Images, Inc.; p. 6 © Tim Shaffer-Pool/Getty Images, Inc.; p. 8 © Jim McIsaac/Getty Images, Inc.; pp. 12, 26 © Stephen Dunn/Getty Images, Inc.; p. 14 © Jonathan Daniel/Getty Images, Inc.; p. 17 © Harry How/Getty Images, Inc.; p. 18 © Jonathan Daniel/Getty Images, Inc.; p. 22 © Ronald Martinez/Getty Images, Inc.; p. 25 © Brian Bahr/Getty Images, Inc.; p. 29 © Doug Benc/Getty Images, Inc.; pp. 32, 35 © Jamie Squire/Getty Images, Inc.; p. 36 © Jonathan Daniel/Getty Images, Inc.; p. 38 © Lisa Blumenfeld/Getty Images, Inc.; p. 41 © Jed Jacobsohn/Getty Images, Inc.

Library of Congress Cataloging-in-Publication Data

Buckman, Virginia.
    Baseball stars / Virginia Buckman.
    p. cm. — (Greatest sports heroes)
    Includes index.
    ISBN-10: 0-531-12583-1 (lib. bdg.)   0-531-18700-4 (pbk.)
    ISBN-13: 978-0-531-12583-0 (lib. bdg.)   978-0-531-18700-5 (pbk.)
    1. Baseball players—United States—Biography—Juvenile literature. I. Title.
    II. Series.
    GV865.A1B855 2007
    796.323092'2—dc22 [B]
                                                        2006014495

1 2 3 4 5 6 7 8 9 10 R 11 10 09 08 07

Contents

Introduction

The rising fastball looks good to you as it approaches the plate. You swing—and miss. "Strike two," yells the umpire. The fans in the crowd groan. "Come on, man, get your head in the game," screams one anxious fan. In disappointment, you hang your head and tap at your cleats with your bat. This is the second time you failed to make contact in this at bat. The first pitch was a change-up that you swung at and missed. With the game on the line, you know you have to come through for the team.

The pitcher goes into his windup and fires his next pitch. It's a sharp curve, breaking away from you. You jump on the pitch and take a good, hard swing. Crack! The sound of the bat meeting the ball echoes over the hushed crowd. As you take off for first base, you keep your eye on the ball as it soars over the right fielder's head. Pulling around first

Major league baseball is made up of the National and the American Leagues. Both have eastern, central, and western division teams.

5

In 1975, the average baseball salary was $45,000.
Today, the average salary is $2.4 million.

base, your heart jumps for joy as the ball clears the fence. A home run! As you round second base, you hear the roar of the crowd. You have helped your team win the game.

Major league baseball players work hard to give fans, teammates, and coaches their best. A baseball player on a major league team can earn a lot of money. With that money, however, comes a lot of pressure to win. The players featured in this book are some of the top baseball talent around. Read on to find out who they are and what makes them tick.

Chapter One

Alex Rodriguez

In 2000, Alex Rodriguez signed with the Texas Rangers for a contract of $252 million over a ten-year period. This was the highest-paying contract ever given to a baseball player. The amount shocked many in the sports community. Many people simply do not agree that any player is worth such a huge amount of money. Today, Alex plays for the New York Yankees, and no one disagrees that he is one of the best ever to play the game.

Early Years

Alex was born in New York City. His family moved to Santo Domingo, the capital of the Dominican Republic, when he was four years old. Alex first began to play baseball in Santo Domingo. When Alex was eight years old, the family moved again, this time to Miami, Florida. Alex's father left the family and moved to New York. It was a difficult time for Alex. His

In June 2005, Alex became the youngest player to hit 400 home runs. He was twenty-nine years old.

mother, Lourdes, was forced to take two jobs to support the family. Alex recalls, "I kept thinking my father would come back, but he never did."

Looking for support in this tough time, Alex joined the Boys and Girls Club. There, his talent for baseball was nurtured. Alex regularly gives credit to the club. "Today, there are three thousand Boys and Girls Clubs where caring people help our children succeed," he says. "Does it work? It did for me."

Developing His Skills

By the time he was in high school, Alex had become a tremendous all-around athlete. He played varsity basketball as a freshman at Christopher Columbus High School in Miami.

Player Stats

Name: Alex Emmanuel Rodriguez

Nickname: A-Rod

Team: New York Yankees

Position: Third Base

Height: 6' 3"

Weight: 225 lbs.

Date of Birth: July 27, 1975

Bats: Right

Throws: Right

In his sophomore year, Alex transferred to Westminster Christian High, where he was starting quarterback of the football team. He was starting shortstop for the baseball team, too. He earned All-American honors in baseball, batting .477 with 6 home runs, 42 stolen bases, and 52 runs in his junior year. Alex won many awards in high school, including the Gatorade National Baseball Student Athlete of the Year.

Hitting the Big Leagues

In 1993, Alex's professional baseball career began when he was the number one overall draft pick. One scouting director said of Alex, "He might be the best player ever in the draft." At just eighteen years old, Alex signed his first major league contract with the Seattle Mariners.

In 1996, Alex played his first full season as starting shortstop. He led the league with a .358 batting average. He had 215 hits, which is the most ever by a shortstop in one season. He also hit 36 home runs. Alex's amazing season earned him the *Sporting News* Major

Alex, along with the rest of Team USA, defeated Japan 4 to 3 in the World Baseball Classic on March 12, 2006.

League Player of the Year award and Associated Press Player of the Year honors. Since then, Alex has earned many awards. Most recently, he was named the American League Most Valuable Player (MVP) for 2005.

A-Rod Gives Back

Alex likes to share his success with people who are less fortunate. He is the national spokesperson for the Boys and Girls Clubs of America. He often holds fund-raising events for the organization. In 2002, he gave $3.9 million to the University of Miami. The money is for a scholarship fund for members of the Boys and Girls Club of Miami. Alex has also begun work on the Alex Rodriguez Learning Center, which will help educate needy children. He donated $200,000 to the Children's Aid Society in Washington Heights, New York, in 2005.

Chapter Two

Dontrelle Willis

Dontrelle Willis is a starting pitcher for the Florida Marlins. He is the type of baseball player who is more excited about playing than getting paid. Despite signing a $4.35 million contract in January 2006, all he could think about was playing for the United States in the World Baseball Classic. "…There is no higher honor than to represent your country," said Willis.

D-Train's Hero

Dontrelle was born in Oakland, California. Dontrelle's mother, Joyce, was a catcher on a top-level softball team. Many of Dontrelle's early memories are of his mom playing softball. She taught him everything about the game. When asked who his hero is, Dontrelle replies, "My mother."

Even as a child, Dontrelle's athletic ability showed through. He holds the home run

In 2005, Dontrelle earned the Warren Spahn Award, which is given to the best left-handed starting pitcher in the league.

record in the Alameda Little League, hitting 15 home runs in one season at the age of twelve. Dontrelle attended Encinal High School in Alameda, California. He was named California High School Player of the Year in 2000. That season Dontrelle struck out 111 batters in seventy innings.

D-Train Rolls Into Florida

In 2000, Dontrelle was drafted by the Chicago Cubs. The Cubs traded him to the Florida Marlins in March 2002. In 2003, Dontrelle was named the National League Rookie of the Year. He went 14-6 with a 2.20 earned run average (ERA) in twenty-seven starts. In the 2005 season, he won a league-leading twenty-two games and finished the season with a 2.63 ERA.

Player Stats

Name: Dontrelle Wayne Willis

Nickname: D-Train

Team: Florida Marlins

Position: Starting Pitcher

Height: 6' 4"

Weight: 239 lbs.

Date of Birth: January 12, 1982

Bats: Left

Throws: Left

Dontrelle's signature move is his high leg kick before pitching the ball.

Helping Others

Dontrelle has become an active fund-raiser for charity. "I just try to do my part. And as I get better career-wise, hopefully my resources get better and I can do more," he told the *Miami Herald.* He has recently begun the Dontrelle Willis Mini-Marlins Tee Ball League. This is a baseball organization for inner-city youth.

Chapter Three

Albert Pujols

Jose Alberto Pujols has always had his eyes on the prize. His plan has always been a simple one: "To try to help my team out to win and hopefully get that ring." The ring that Albert is aiming for is the one given to the champions of the World Series. It is the ultimate goal of any baseball player. The ring is a symbol of all the hard work and training needed to be the best. Albert came close to his goal in 2004. That year the Saint Louis Cardinals went to the World Series, but came up short against the Boston Red Sox.

Young Prince Albert

Albert Pujols was born in Santo Domingo, Dominican Republic. His family moved to the United States, eventually settling in Independence, Missouri. Pujols batted over .500 in his first season playing baseball at Fort Osage High School. Albert received a baseball

Albert Pujols was picked to be a part of the 2005 Latino Legends Team, an all-star baseball game honoring Latin-American baseball players.

scholarship to Maple Woods Community College. He was a standout as a college player, batting .461 in his first season.

Rising Through the Ranks

The Saint Louis Cardinals drafted Pujols in 1999. Albert was disappointed with their offer and turned it down. That summer he played for the Jayhawk League in Kansas, hoping to sharpen his skills and improve his value. The Cardinals soon came back with a better offer, and Albert signed with them at the end of summer.

In 2000, Albert played with the Peoria Chiefs of the Midwest League. Albert posted an impressive season and was voted the League's Most Valuable Player. He went on to play for the Potomac Cannons and then the

Player Stats

Name: Jose Alberto Pujols

Nickname: Prince Albert

Team: Saint Louis Cardinals

Position: First Base

Height: 6' 3"

Weight: 225 lbs.

Date of Birth: January 16, 1980

Bats: Right

Throws: Right

Memphis Redbirds. After only seven games as a Redbird, Pujols was hitting .367 and had 2 home runs.

In the Majors

In 2001, Albert posted one of the finest rookie seasons in major league baseball (MLB) history. He batted a team-leading .329 and pounded in 130 RBIs on 194 hits. Albert earned National League Rookie of the Year honors. He also finished fourth in the National League Most Valuable Player voting. Such an honor is almost unheard of for a rookie.

Albert's success continued through the following seasons. In 2003, he batted .359 with 43 home runs and 124 RBIs. He was named Major League Player of the Year by the *Sporting News* for the season's performance. Albert was named the National League Most Valuable Player in 2005. Also, he is the first player in major league history to hit 30 or more home runs in each of his first five seasons.

Chapter Four

Roy Oswalt

Some players play for the love of the game. Others play for money. Roy Oswalt, oddly enough, actually played for a bulldozer. When Astros owner Drayton McLane asked Roy Oswalt about his goals, Oswalt declared that he had always wanted to own a bulldozer. "That kind of took me back a little bit. I had never heard that before," said McLane.

McLane made a promise to Oswalt: If Roy did his part in beating the Saint Louis Cardinals in the 2005 National League play-offs, the owner promised he would buy Oswalt an all-purpose tractor. When the Astros beat the Cardinals, McLane made good on his promise. "There are going to be a lot of jealous people around where I live," Oswalt said about his new Caterpillar D6N XL.

Developing His Skills

Roy Oswalt was born in Weir, Mississippi. Roy was a great pitcher in college. He earned

Roy and the rest of the Astros went to the World Series in 2005. This was the first time the Astros ever played in the World Series.

All-American honors pitching at Galveston Community College. In 1996, Roy was drafted by the Houston Astros.

Roy made his major league debut in 2001. He went 14-3 and posted a 2.73 ERA. Roy also struck out 144 batters in 141 innings pitched. His performance earned him the Sporting News National League Pitcher Rookie of the Year Award. Roy kept rolling strong in 2002, posting a 19-9 season with a 3.01 ERA.

The Payoff

In February 2004, Roy signed a $16.9 million contract for two more years with the Astros. He has posted consecutive twenty-win seasons and helped lead the Astros to the 2005 World Series. Roy was voted the

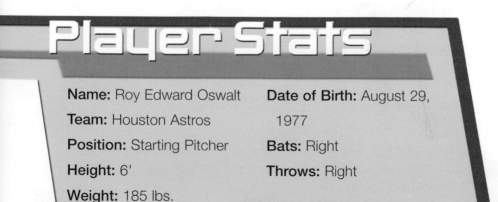

Player Stats

Name: Roy Edward Oswalt

Team: Houston Astros

Position: Starting Pitcher

Height: 6'

Weight: 185 lbs.

Date of Birth: August 29, 1977

Bats: Right

Throws: Right

Early in the 2006 season, Roy pitched fifteen winning games in a row against the Cincinnati Reds.

National League Championship Series' Most Valuable Player in 2005. "The best thing about the whole thing was to give the trophy to my dad after the celebration," he said, "just because growing up, he was never late coming home to get me to a ballgame…"

Roy's career stats are an impressive 83-39 win/loss record with a 3.07 ERA. The Astros believe that Roy has the potential to become the best pitcher in the league.

Chapter Five

Eric Gagne

Eric Gagne (**gahn**-yay) has always been outspoken about his desire to be a champion. During the 2005 season, Eric shared his plan to help the Dodgers win more games. "You need to add a 40 home run guy and a guy who hits .310." Gagne clearly wanted the Dodgers to spend more to get quality players. He explained, "The Dodgers make money. The fans show up. You have to give back. As a business, you have to make money. But you have to take risks to make money, and in baseball that means paying for players."

Heading into the 2006 season, Gagne is as vocal as ever. He recently stated that if the Dodgers did not shape up he would not hesitate to find a new team. "I close games; I can't save losses," he told the *Los Angeles Times*. Only a very confident player can make such statements. As one of the best closing pitchers in Dodgers' history, Eric has plenty to be confident about.

Before coming to the United States for college, Eric spoke only French.

Growing Up Gagne

Eric Gagne was raised in Mascouche, Canada. As a child, his parents encouraged him to participate in sports. In addition to baseball, Eric enjoyed playing hockey. Eric grew up watching the Expos play at Olympic Stadium and dreamed of becoming a major league player. He attended Polyvalente Edouard Montpetit High School, where he played hockey and baseball.

Playing the Game

Eric's path to the major leagues was not an easy one. After a successful first season in the minor leagues, Eric was forced to undergo surgery on his throwing arm. Eric came back

Player Stats

Name: Eric Serge Gagne

Team: Los Angeles Dodgers

Position: Relief Pitcher

Height: 6' 2"

Weight: 234 lbs.

Date of Birth: January 7, 1976

Bats: Right

Throws: Right

Eric has to wear goggles to protect his eyes because of an eye injury he got while playing hockey when he was younger.

strong from the surgery, and two seasons later was named Dodger Minor League Pitcher of the Year in 1999. Later that year, he was called up to play for the Dodgers.

Since his major league debut in 1999, Eric has developed into one of the best closers in the game. After an impressive 2002 season, Eric really hit his stride in the 2003 season. He posted an amazing 1.20 ERA—the lowest ever among major league pitchers with seventy-five or more appearances in a single season. Eric simply shut down the batters of

Baseball for the Blind

Baseball is a game of skill, but not necessarily a game of sight. The National Beep Baseball Association has created a unique form of baseball that can be played by the blind. The game uses sounds to help the players locate the ball and the bases. The bases contain buzzing units that make sounds when activated. The ball beeps so that players can locate its position. The pitcher and the catcher are the only sighted players on the teams.

every team he pitched against. His 2003 performance earned him the National League Cy Young Award.

Pitching In

Off the field, Eric donates his time and money to helping out his community. In 2003 and 2004, he set up a program to raise money for the UCLA Children's Hospital Cancer Research Foundation. Eric has worked to promote National Hunger Awareness Day, Dodgers Dream Foundation, and the Jonsson Comprehensive Cancer Center.

Miguel Tejada

It is not often that the arrival of a single player can re-energize a team, but for Miguel Tejada that was exactly the case. "This franchise changed the day he arrived," Orioles' hitting instructor Terry Crowley said. Miguel Tejada plays shortstop for the Baltimore Orioles. Fellow teammate Brian Roberts feels that Tejada is the best shortstop in the league. Roberts explains, "He has an uncanny ability to knock in runs. He is always up, pushing everyone and making the entire team better."

Discovering Miguel

Miguel was born in Bani, Dominican Republic. He dreamed of playing professional baseball. Miguel eventually realized his dream through hard work and determination. While playing baseball as a teenager, his abilities attracted the interest of scouts. Juan Marichal, a scout for the Oakland Athletics, signed Miguel as a

Miguel won the Century 21 Home Run Derby in July 2004.

free agent in July 1993. Miguel was just seventeen years old. He began playing the following season.

A Big Bird

In 1998, Miguel became starting shortstop for the Oakland A's. Miguel had a solid rookie season. He hit 20 home runs, 20 doubles, and scored 53 runs. These numbers put Miguel among the top five American League rookies. In 1999, he pounded in 84 RBIs and 21 home runs. By 2001, his home run total had soared to 31. After an amazing season in 2002, Miguel was named the American League's Most Valuable Player.

Miguel's MVP award put him among baseball's elite players. It also earned him a

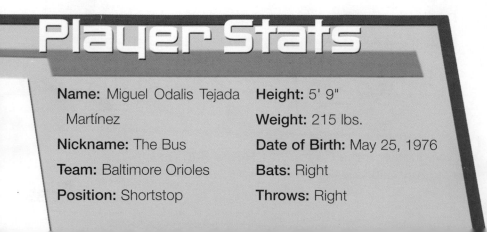

Player Stats

Name: Miguel Odalis Tejada Martínez

Nickname: The Bus

Team: Baltimore Orioles

Position: Shortstop

Height: 5' 9"

Weight: 215 lbs.

Date of Birth: May 25, 1976

Bats: Right

Throws: Right

Here Miguel makes a double play over Jonny Gomes of the Devil Rays.

great deal of money. In 2003, the Baltimore Orioles awarded Miguel with a seventy-two million dollar contract. Miguel's arrival in Baltimore was celebrated by Oriole fans. He is the type of player who can lead a team to championships.

Tejada Speaks

Miguel's career has not been free of controversy. He has drawn unwanted attention from the press. In December 2005, news

Miguel displays his MVP trophy of the seventy-sixth Major League Baseball All-Star Game at Comerica Park in July 2005.

reports stated that Miguel had asked the Orioles for a trade. Miguel challenged these reports, saying that the press misinterpreted his words. He claimed that he did not want to leave the Orioles, but that he just wanted the Orioles to be a better team. Some people feel that Miguel is justified in demanding to win more games. Others feel that a good teammate should not speak to the press in such a way that it disturbs team chemistry.

Miguel the Man

Only gifted athletes can accomplish what Miguel has in his career. Miguel is a special person off the field as well. He does not forget his roots and likes to help those less fortunate. Instead of celebrating his new fortune when he signed with the Orioles, Miguel and his family spent time helping hurricane victims in the Dominican Republic. Also, he had a three thousand seat stadium built in Bani, his hometown.

Chapter Seven

Vladimir Guerrero

Vladimir Guerrero was born in Nizao Bani, Dominican Republic. His family was very poor, so he stopped going to school after the fifth grade to support his family. Vlad learned early on that only hard work could improve his family's life. Luckily for Vlad, he had athletic gifts to go along with his strong work ethic. His baseball talent was noticed by scouts, and he was offered a contract to play for the Montreal Expos in 1993.

He has come a long way since those early years. In 2004, he was named the American League's Most Valuable Player. In September 2005, Vladimir Guerrero became one of only eleven players in major league history to hit 300 home runs before the age of thirty.

Playing in the Big Leagues

Vlad was voted a minor league all-star three times. In 1996, after just three years in the minors, Vlad moved up to play in the major

Vladimir has played on the All-Star team six times. He is known for being an aggressive swinger.

leagues. Vlad played seven seasons with the Expos. By 2000, Vlad had become a home run hitting machine. He hit more than 40 home runs in back-to-back seasons. Vlad's aggressive batting style had made him one of the most feared players in the game. In 2002, Vlad was named the Expos' Most Valuable Player for the fourth time.

To the Victor Go the Spoils

In 2004, Vlad signed a five-year, seventy million dollar contract with the Los Angeles Angels of Anaheim. Vlad batted .337, knocked in 126 RBIs, and slugged 39 home runs. In the final seven games of the season, Vlad turned in one of the best hitting streaks in baseball history. He batted .536 with 6 home runs and 11 RBIs.

Player Stats

Name: Vladimir Alvino Guerrero

Nickname: Vlad the Impaler

Team: Los Angeles Angels

Position: Right Field

Height: 6' 3"

Weight: 225 lbs.

Date of Birth: February 9, 1976

Bats: Right

Throws: Right

Vlad's amazing performance in the 2004 season sealed him the spot as the American League Most Valuable Player.

Helping Out at Home

Vlad regularly returns to the Dominican Republic to share his riches with his fellow Dominicans. He has started a number of businesses to provide Dominicans with jobs. These businesses include a cement-block factory and a supermarket.

While back home, Vlad cannot help but think of his past. Vlad recalls, " I still do a lot of the things I did as a kid, (but) at least I don't have to drink from the puddles anymore."

New Words

American League (uh-**mer**-uh-kuhn **leeg**) one of the two leagues in major league baseball; the champion team of the American League meets the champion team of the National League in the World Series

batting average (**bat**-ihng **av**-uh-ij) the average amount of times a player gets a hit while at bat

closer (**kloz**-uhr) a pitcher whose job is to save games; a closer can be brought in when a team is ahead late in a game to preserve the lead

consecutive (kuhn-**sek**-yuh-tiv) happening or following one after the other

controversy (**kon**-truh-vur-see) an argument

draft (**draft**) the process that major league baseball teams use to select players to join their organizations

earned run average (**urnd run av**-uh-ij) a measure of how well a pitcher performs

New Words

free agent (**free ay**-jent) in baseball, a player
  who is free to sign a contract with any team

National League (**nash**-uh-nuhl **leeg**) one of the
  two leagues in Major League Baseball; the
  champion team of the National League meets
  the champion team of the American League in
  the World Series

nurtured (**nur**-churd) helped someone or
  something to grow

professional (pruh-**fesh**-uh-nuhl) making money
  for doing something that others do for fun

runs batted in (**runz bat**-uhd **in**) when a player
  causes a run to be scored by hitting the ball
  into play

shortstop (**short**-stop) in baseball or softball, the
  player whose position is between the second
  and third bases

For Further Reading

January, Brendan. *A Baseball All-Star.*
Portsmouth, NH: Heinemann, 2004.

Kahn, Roger, and Murray Tinkelman.
*The Head Game: Baseball Seen from the
Pitcher's Mound.* Orlando, FL: Harcourt, 2000.

Ross, Dalton. *Top Teams Ever: Football,
Baseball, Basketball, and Hockey Winners.*
New York: Rosen Publishing Group, 2002.

Schmidt, Julie. *Satchel Paige.* New York:
Rosen Publishing Group, 2002.

Young, Jeff C. *Top 10 World Series MVPs.*
Berkeley Heights, NJ: Enslow, 2001.

Resources

ORGANIZATIONS

American Amateur Baseball Congress (AABC)
National Office
100 West Broadway
Farmington, NM 87401
(505) 327-3120
www.aabc.us

National Baseball Hall of Fame and Museum
25 Main Street
Cooperstown, NY 13326
(888) HALL-OF-FAME or (888) 425-5633
www.baseballhalloffame.org

Resources

WEB SITES

Baseball Almanac
www.baseball-almanac.com
This site has much information about the history of baseball.

Baseball America ESPN
www.baseballamerica.com/today/index.html
From high school to the draft, find out everything newsworthy in baseball.

Exploratorium: The Science of Baseball
www.exploratorium.edu/baseball
The Museum of Science, Art, and Human Perception offers this Web site of fun and fact.

Major League Baseball
http://mlb.mlb.com
Visit this Web site for news, player biographies, and much major league baseball information.

Index

Index

ABOUT THE AUTHOR

Virginia Buckman has written numerous books on a wide variety of nonfiction subjects. She currently lives and works in New York City.